EASY TO PLAY COUNTRY GUITAR

BY WILLIAM BAY, TOMMY FLINT, STEVE GRIFFIN AND ROGER FILIBERTO

Visit us on the Web at www.melbay.com or www.billsmusicshelf.com

TUNING THE GUITAR

The six open strings of the guitar are of the same pitch as the six notes shown in the illustration of the piano keyboard. Note that five of the strings are below the middle C of the piano keyboard.

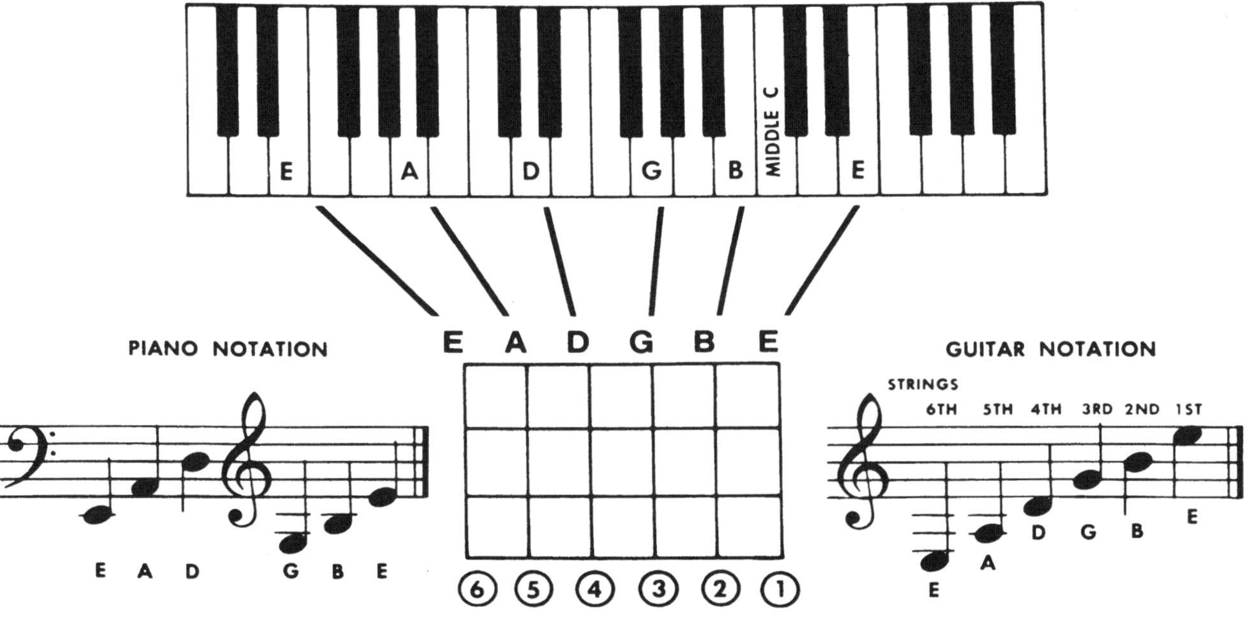

Another Method of Tuning

1. **Tune the sixth string in unison to the E or 12th white key to the LEFT of MIDDLE C on the piano.**
2. **Place your finger behind the 5th fret of the sixth string. This will give you the tone or pitch of the fifth string (A).**
3. **Place your finger behind the 5th fret of the fifth string to get the pitch of the fourth string (D).**
4. **Repeat the same procedure to obtain the pitch of the third string (G).**
5. **Place your finger behind the 4TH FRET of the third string to get the pitch of the second string (B).**
6. **Place your finger behind the 5th fret of the second string to get the pitch of the first string (E).**

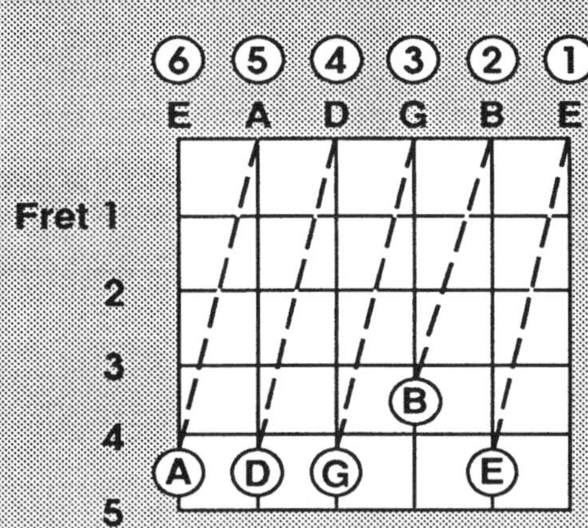

ELECTRONIC TUNERS

Electronic tuners come in many forms and are a great way to tune your guitar. They will give you a visual display showing whether each string is sharp or flat. You can buy them at your local music store.

Explanation of Symbols Used

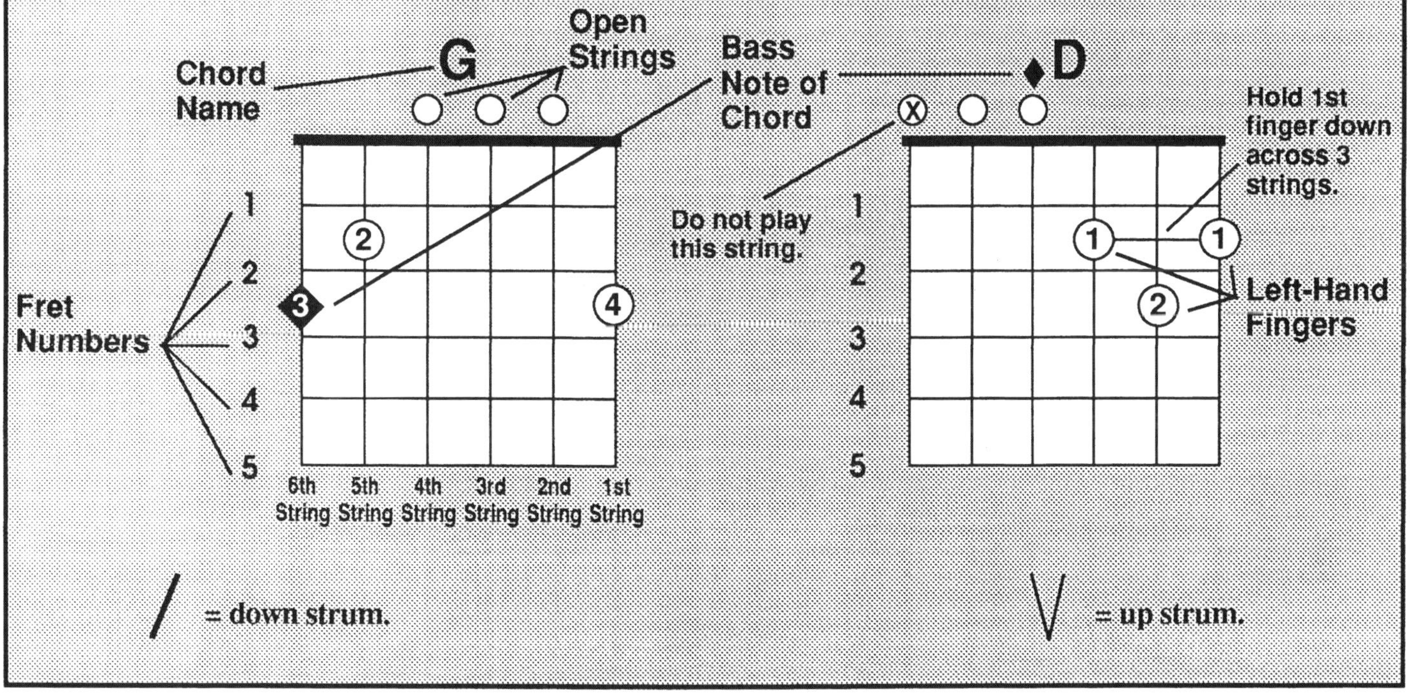

Chord Name

G

Open Strings

Bass Note of Chord

D

Hold 1st finger down across 3 strings.

Fret Numbers 1 2 3 4 5

Do not play this string.

Left-Hand Fingers

6th String 5th String 4th String 3rd String 2nd String 1st String

/ = down strum.

V = up strum.

Time Signatures

C or $\frac{4}{4}$ — 4 (4 beats per measure.) 4 (A quarter note receives one beat.) Count: 1-2-3-4, 1-2-3-4, etc.	2 (2 beats per measure.) 4 (A quarter note receives one beat.) Count: 1-2, 1-2, etc.
3 (3 beats per measure.) 4 (A quarter note receives one beat.) Count: 1-2-3, 1-2-3, etc.	6 (6 beats per measure.) 8 (An eighth note receives one beat.) Count: **1**-2-3-**4**-5-6, **1**-2-3-**4**-5-6, etc. (Accent beats 1 and 4.)

HOLDING THE PICK

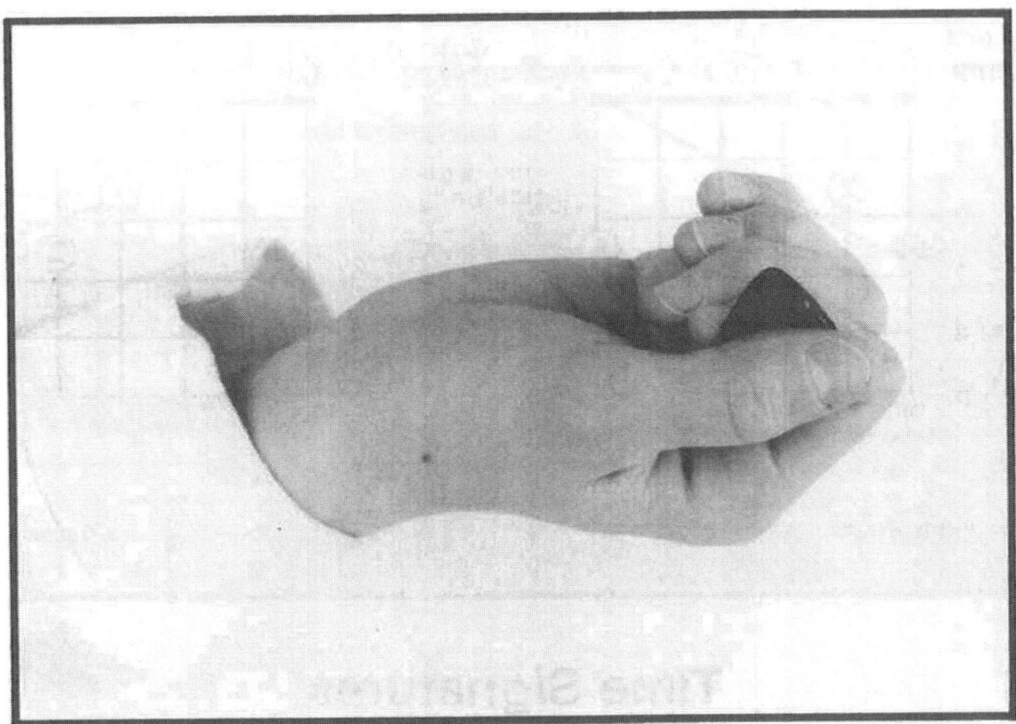

Now is the time to introduce the used of the flatpick. Study the photograph carefully; make certain that the pick is not held too tightly. Practice strumming up and down with the flatpick in order to get the feel of it. Take careful note of the symbols used to denote down pick and up pick. This will be used throughout.

Check your hand position. Do not hold the pick too tightly!

/ **= down strum.**

V **= up strum.**

Chords in G

The three basic chords in the key of G are: G, C, and D7. A diamond ◆ indicates the bass or tonic note of a chord.

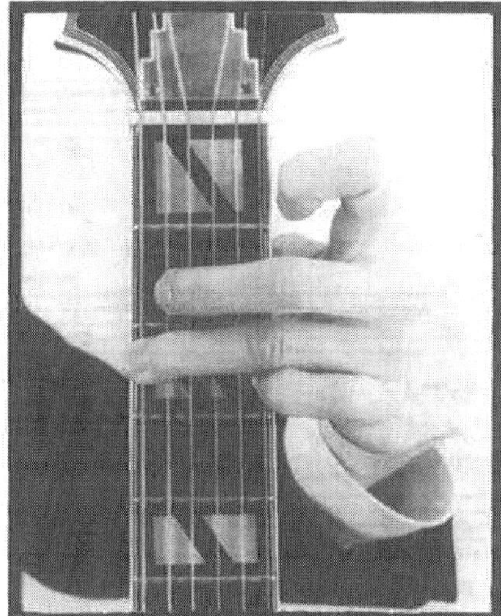

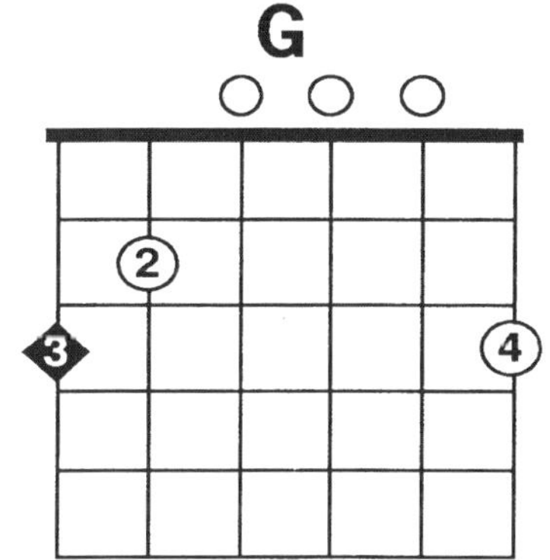

If fingering the G chord is difficult, omit the bottom two strings and play only the top four.

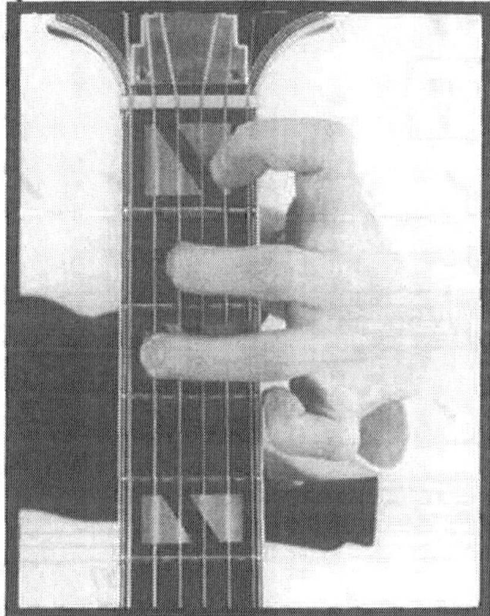

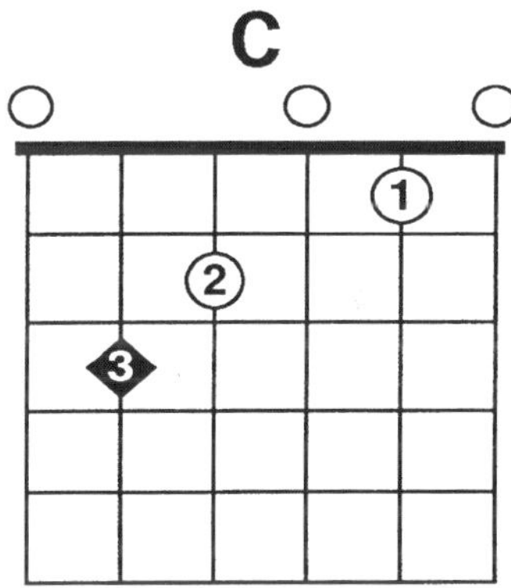

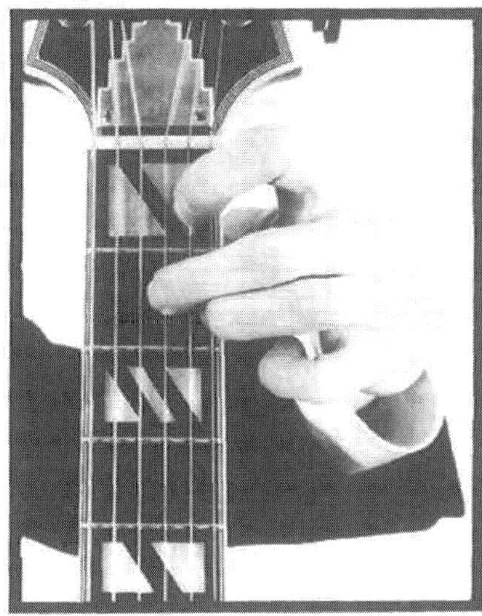

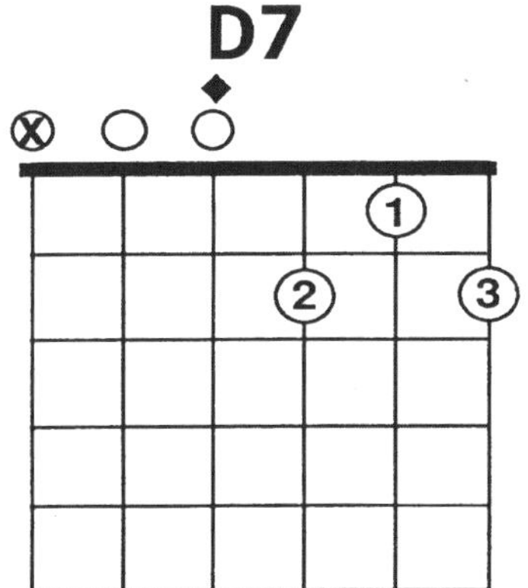

(The *bass note* is the fourth string played open.)

Peace Like a River
Starting Pitch
Strum Down Down Down up Down up
G C D7
1. I've got peace like a riv - er, I've got peace like a riv - er, I've got peace like a riv - er in my soul; I've got peace like a riv - er I've got peace like a riv - er, I've got peace like a riv - er in my soul.
2. I've got joy like a fountain
3. I've got love like an ocean.
I Never Will Marry
Starting Pitch
Strum Down Down Down up
Chorus
I nev - er will mar - ry, nor be no man's wife, I ex - pect to stay sin - gle, all the days of my
shells in the o - cean will be my death bed; The fish in deep wa - ter swim o - ver my
1. life The
2. head.
1. One day as I rambled down by the seashore,
The wind it did whistle and the waters did roar.
I spied a fair damsel make a pitiful cry,
It sounded so lonesome in the waters nearby.
Chorus
2. My love's gone and left me, he's the one I adore,
He's gone where I never shall see him any more.
She plunged her dear body in the water so deep,
She closed her pretty blue eyes in the waters to sleep.
Chorus

She'll Be Coming Round the Mountain

Starting Pitch
Strum Down Rest Down up Down up Down up
G
She'll be com - ing round the mountain when she comes, She'll be
D7
com-ing round the moun-tain when she comes, She'll be
G C D7
com - ing round the moun-tain, She'll be com - ing round the moun-tain, She'll be
G D7 G
com - ing round the moun-tain when she comes.

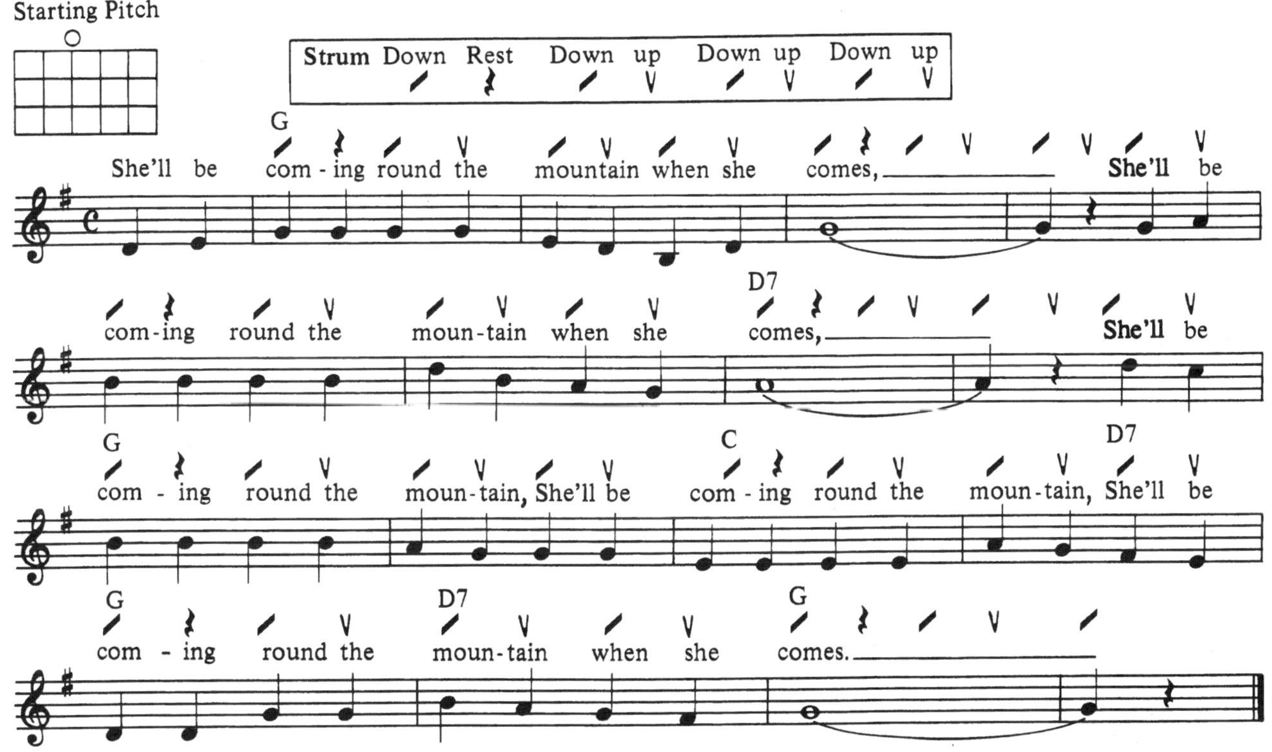

The Gospel Train

Starting Pitch
Strum Down Rest Down up Down up Down up
G C D7
1. The gos - pel train's a com - in', I hear it just at hand, I
G C G D7 G
hear the wheel a mov - 'in and rumb - lin' thro' the land.
Chorus
Get on
C G
board, lit - tle chil - dren; Get on board, lit - tle chil - dren; Get on
C G D7 G
board, lit - tle chil - dren, there's room for man - y a more!

G
2. The fare is cheap and all can go,
C D7
The rich and poor are there;
G C
No second class aboard this train,
G D7 G
No difference in the fare. Chorus

G
3. I hear that train a-comin',
C D7
She sure is speedin' fast,
G C
So get your tickets ready
G D7 G
And ride to heaven at last. Chorus

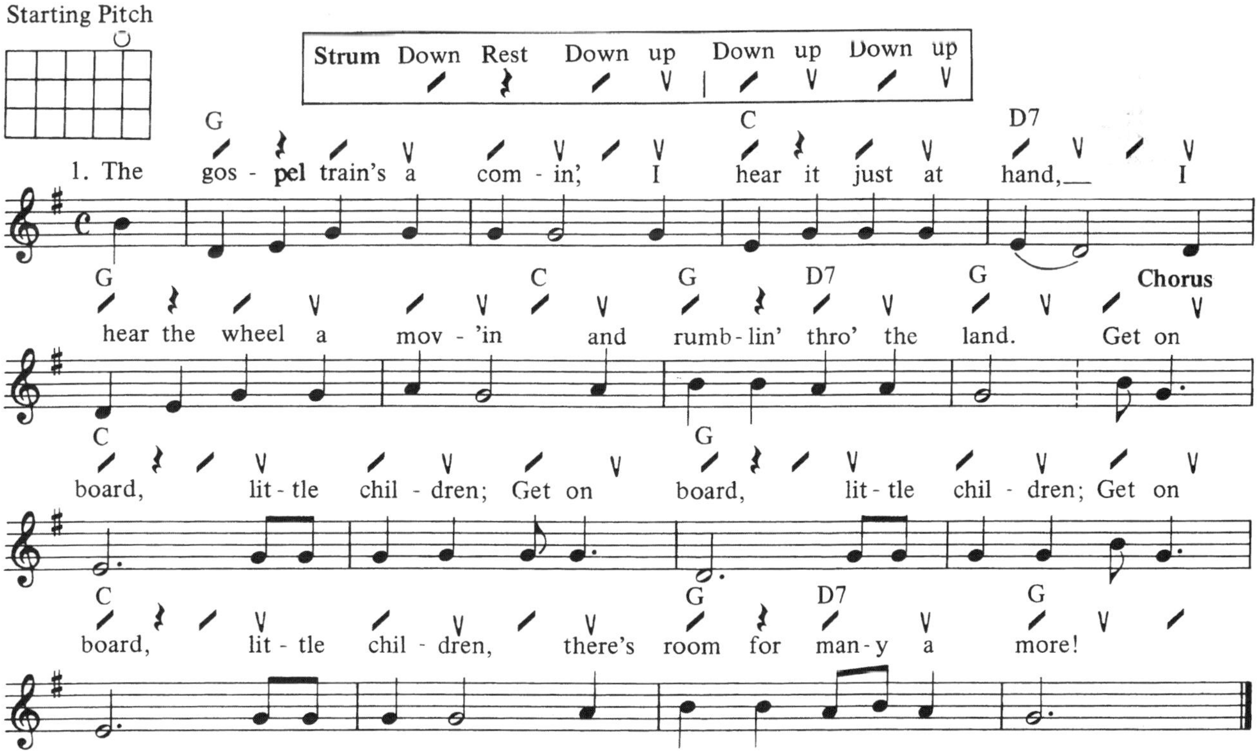

LEARNING TO READ TABLATURE

Tablature is a way of writing guitar music which tells you where to find notes. In tablature:

Lines = Strings

Numbers = Frets

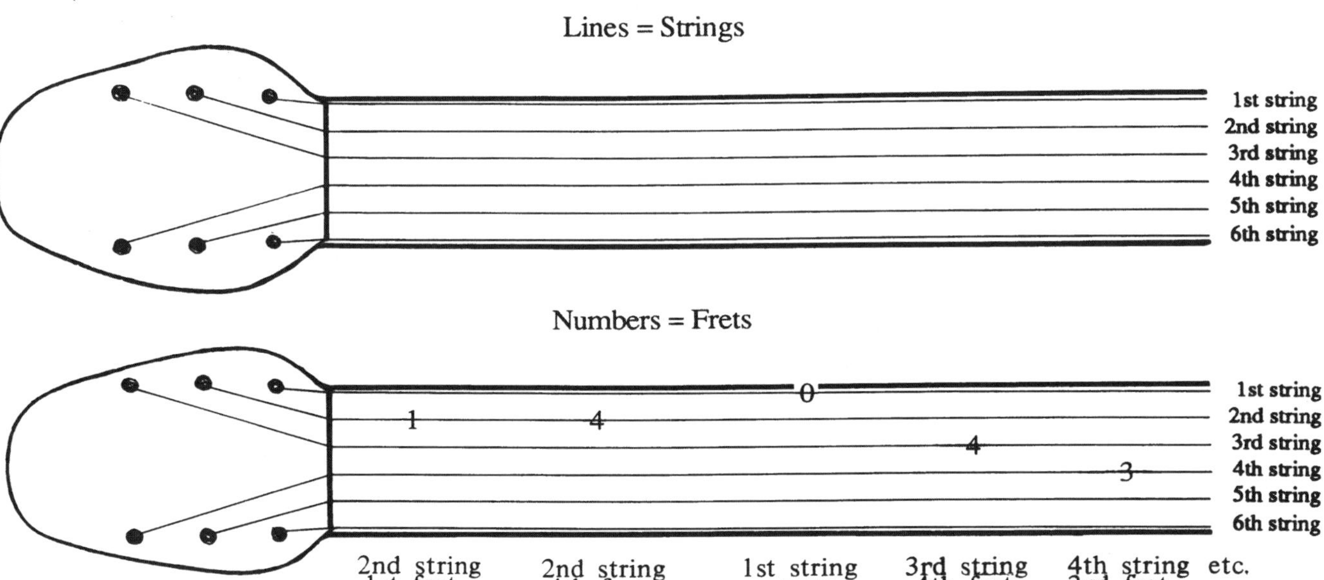

When numbers appear right above one another, more than one note is played at the same time.

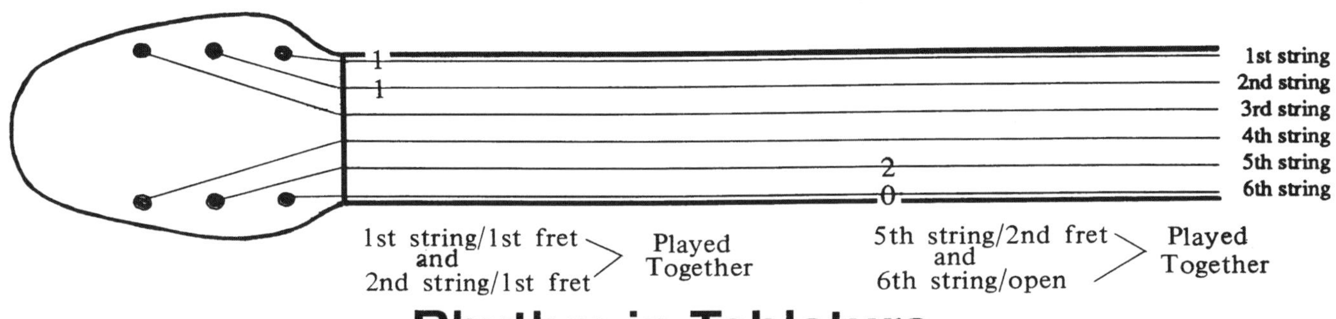

Rhythm in Tablature

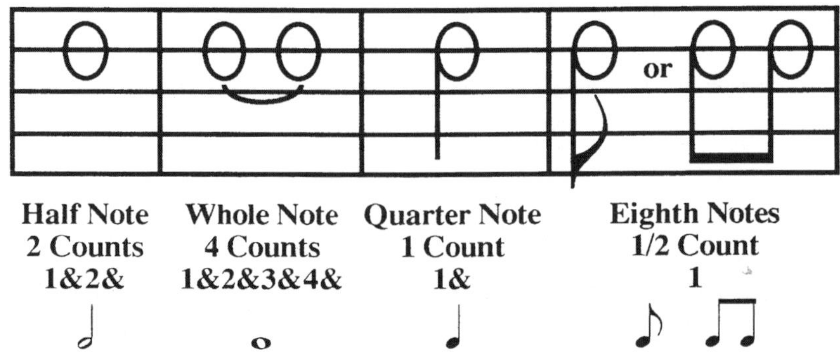

Strum Picking

On the following songs, you will learn a style called "strum picking" which will allow you to combine melody and accompaniment.

Cider Through a Straw

Amazing Grace

Cripple Creek

Bass-Run Accompaniment

The following pieces feature a common country guitar accompaniment technique known as the bass run.

Cowboy Jack

Moderato

Traditional

Cielito Lindo

Mexican Love Song

Look Down That Lonely Road

Country Guitar Solos

The following songs represent a variety of country and bluegrass solo guitar stylings.

Butler County Breakdown

Brightly

Tommy Flint

G7
C
G7
D7
G7
C
D7
F
G7
C
F
C

The Laurel Mountains

Tommy Flint

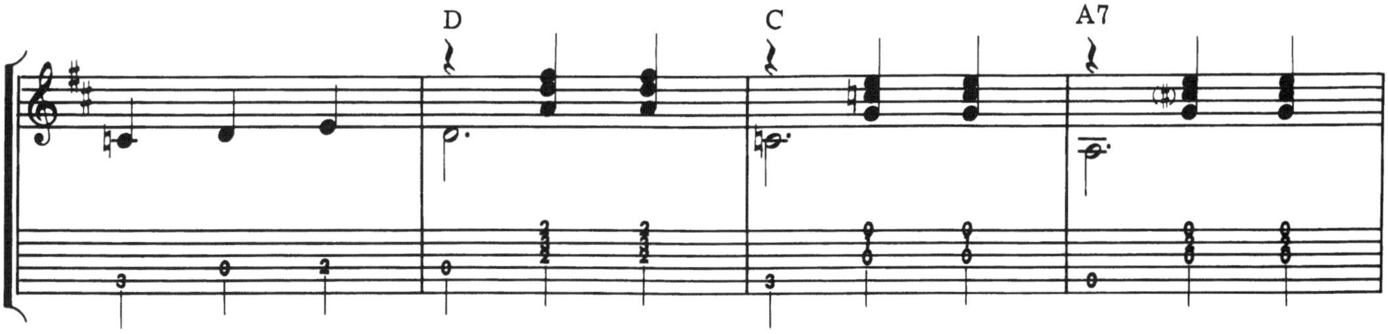
D
C
A7

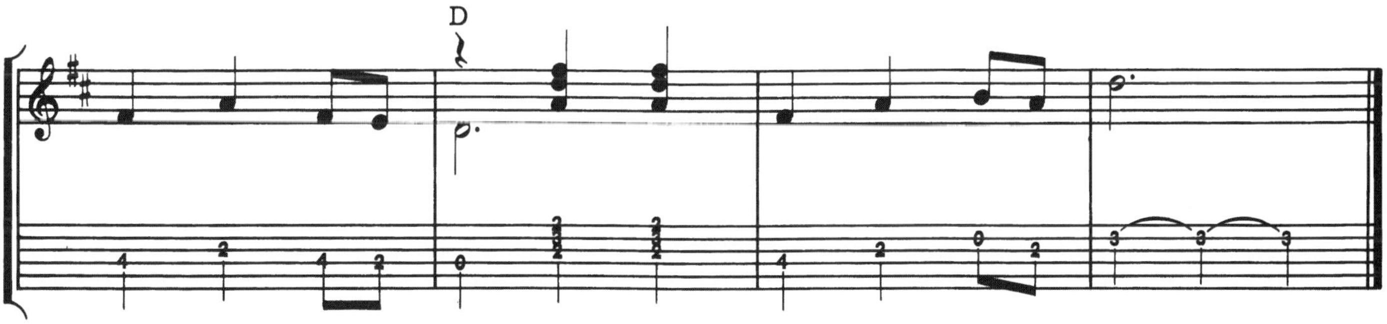
D

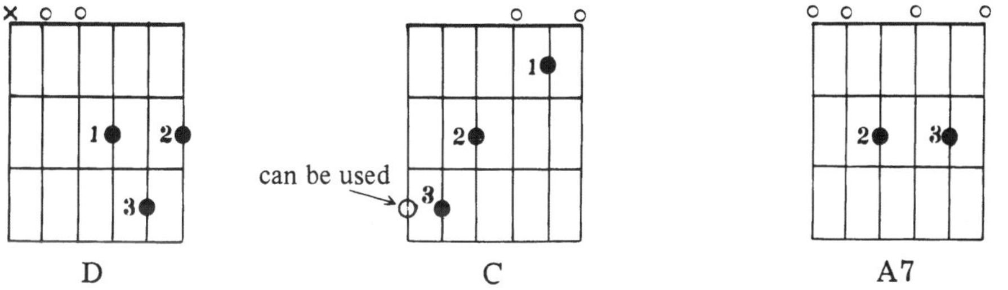
can be used
D
C
A7

Turkey Buzzard

Tommy Flint

Fast

C
G7

C
G7
C

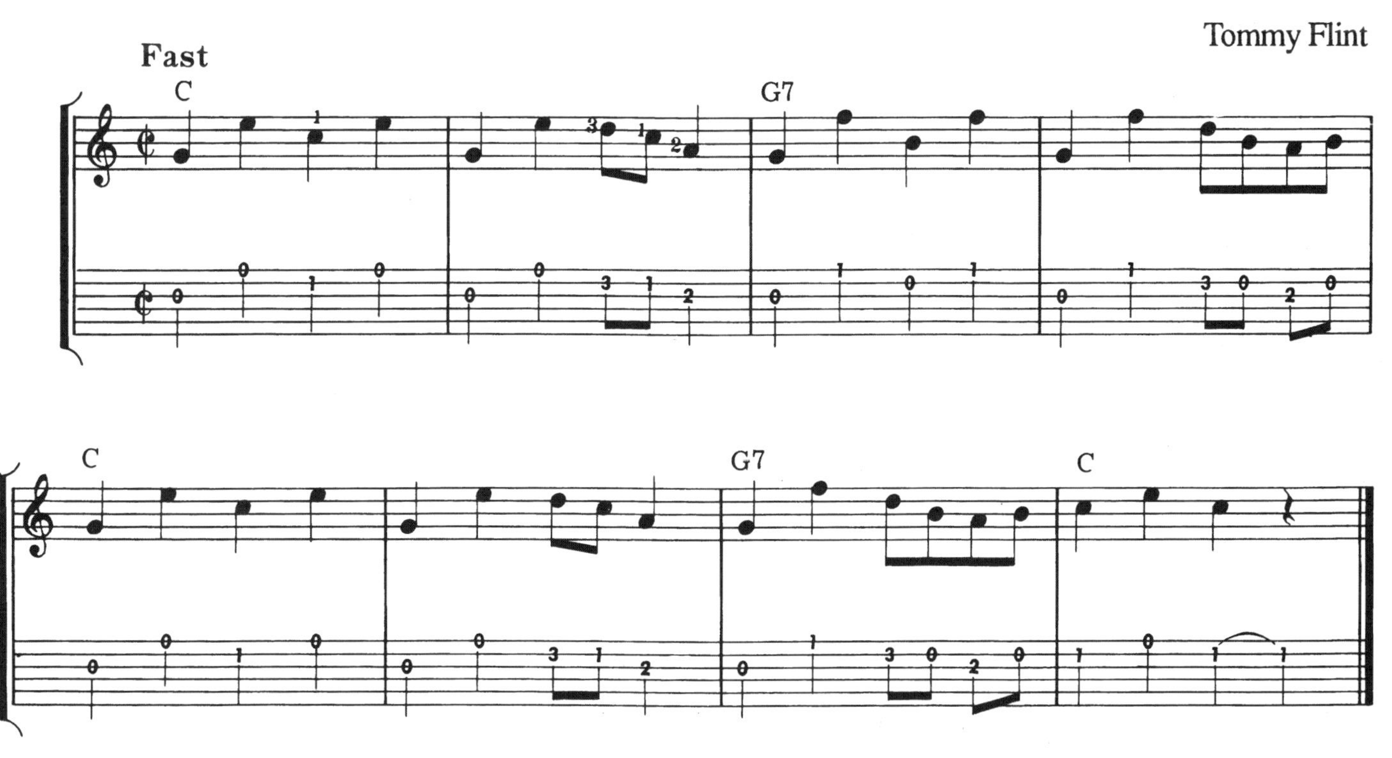

Sally Goodin

Arr. Tommy Flint

*The first B note in measure 5 is played on the third string at the 4th fret.

The line means to slide into the note. Place the finger one or two frets lower (2nd or 3rd fret) and slide rapidly to the 4th fret on the count of one.

Old Joe Clark

Can be played this way:
Eighth notes may be used instead of the quarter notes. Alternate picking should be used. The chords will still be played as quarter notes.

CHORD

Major Key | Relative Minor

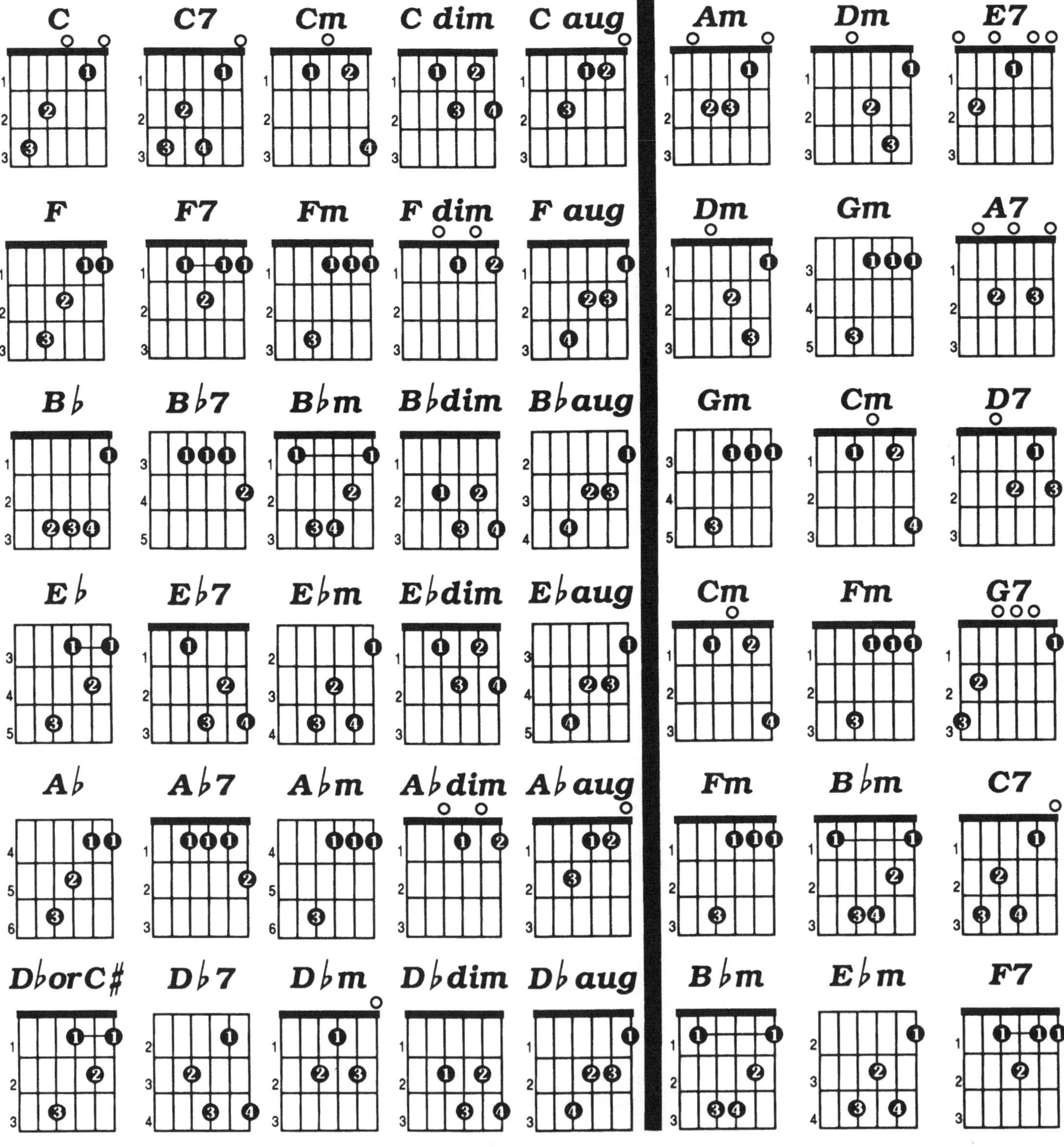

CHART

Major Key | Relative Minor

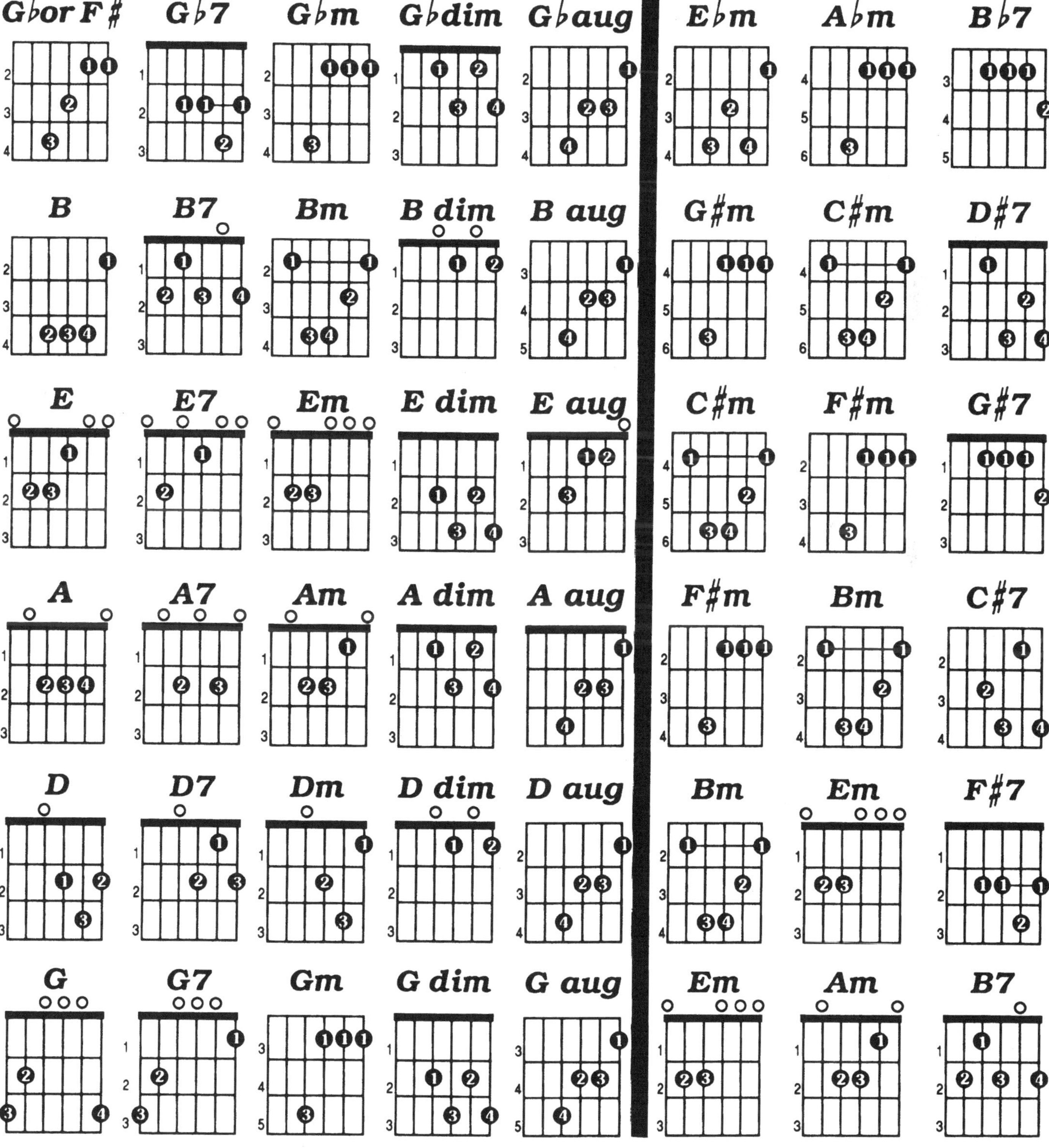

Mr. Peale's Ram

Tommy Flint

Made in the USA
Charleston, SC
25 April 2011